SEASONS

Winter

by Mari Schuh

Kaleidoscope
Minneapolis, MN

Where the Quest for Discovery Begins

This edition first published in 2024 by Kaleidoscope Publishing, Inc.

Kaleidoscope Publishing, Inc.
6012 Blue Circle Drive
Minnetonka, MN 55343

Library of Congress Control Number
2023936903

ISBN
978-1-64519-719-5 (library bound)
978-1-64519-767-6 (ebook)

Bigfoot Jr. lurks within one of the images in this book. It's up to you to find him!

Table of Contents

Winter Is Here!

Snowflakes fall on Rima and her dad as they walk home. "Dad, it's snowing!" she says.

"A **blizzard** is coming. The weather will be windy and cold. Winter is here for sure!" Dad says.

FUN FACT

Winter is the coldest season.

Snow falls in winter. The **temperature** drops. *Brrr!* It is cold outside!

FUN FACT

Water freezes at 32 degrees Fahrenheit (0 degrees Celsius).

Icicles hang from roofs in winter.
Ice forms on lakes and ponds.

Earth's seasons are spring, summer, fall, and winter. Winter is the coldest season.

FUN FACT
Days are shorter in winter.

Winter has fewer hours of sunlight than summer.

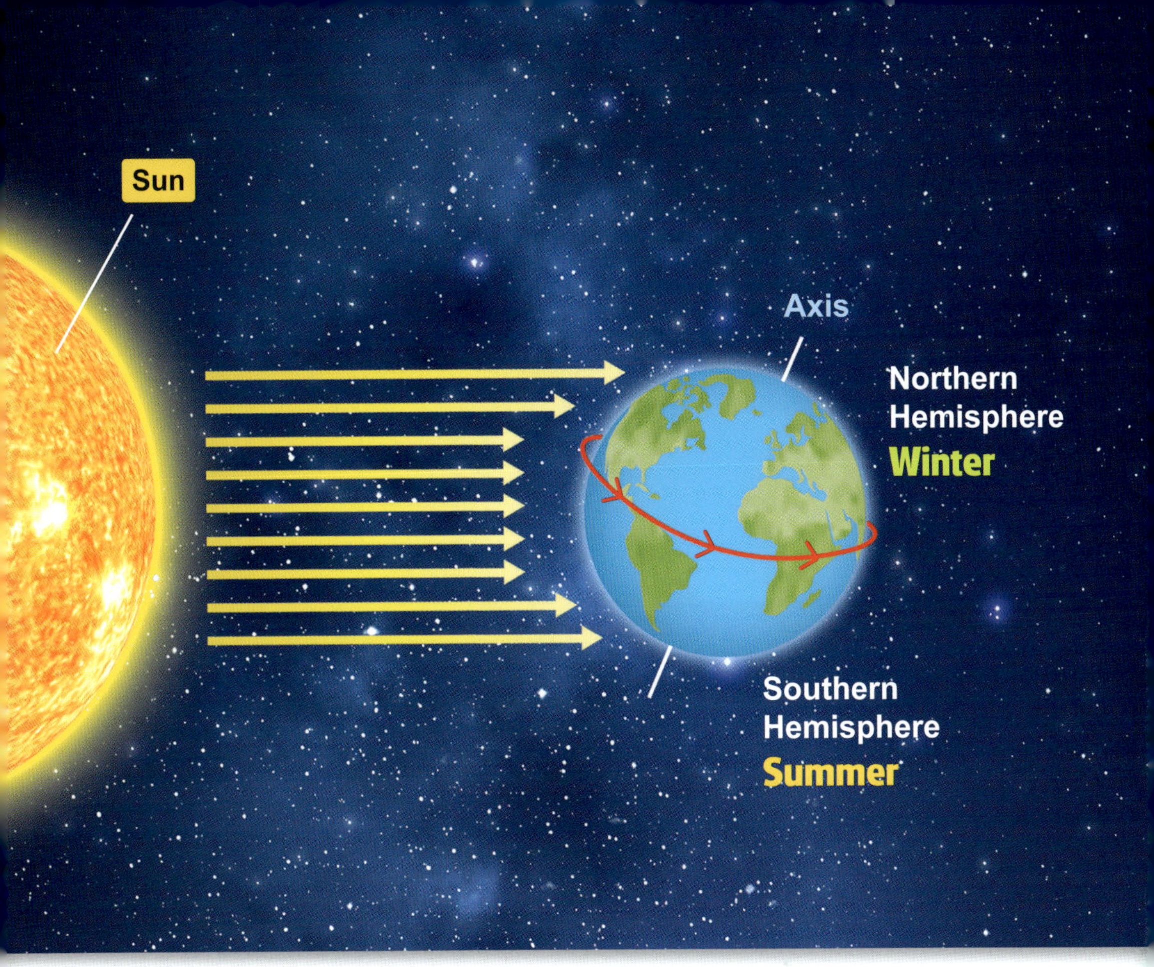

Earth **tilts** as it spins on its **axis**. As Earth travels around the Sun, some areas get more sunlight. When Earth's northern half tilts away from the Sun, it gets less sunlight. Then it is winter on the northern half.

Winter Is Fun!

People move their arms and legs in the snow. They make snow angels!

Many people enjoy the snow in winter. They go skiing. They make snowmen.

In some areas, winter is not very cold. There is no snow. The weather is mild, cool, dry, or hot.

In cold areas, people enjoy hockey and ice fishing. They go sledding and ice skating.

What Do People
Use During Cold Winters?

What do you use in winter?

Animals Get Ready

Fluffy tails keep arctic foxes warm. They use their tail like a blanket.

Arctic foxes grow thick fur to stay warm. The new white fur is **camouflage**. It blends in with the snow.

There is less food in winter. So some animals **hibernate**. Groundhogs sleep in **burrows** under the ground.

Bears spend winter in their **dens**. Some bears come out to look for food.

In winter, box turtles hibernate for three months or more!

Frogs find places to rest all winter. They hide in leaves and logs. They rest in burrows under the ground.

Trees in Winter

Many trees rest in winter. These trees are **dormant**. They do not grow leaves in winter.

The bare trees save their energy. Bark on their trunks protects them from the cold.

FUN FACT
Some flowers bloom in winter!

"I can't see our trees or the street very well, Dad. I'm glad we got home before the big blizzard," Rima says.

"Me too. Blizzards can last many days. We are safe and warm. Let's play a game!" Dad says.

Snowplows are busy in winter. They clear snow from roads and highways.

Photo Glossary

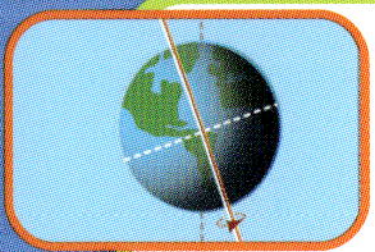

axis: An imaginary line through the center of Earth. Earth spins on its axis. One spin is one day.

blizzard: A big snowstorm. Blizzards have strong winds and lots of snow.

burrows: Holes or tunnels in the ground made or used by small animals. Groundhogs dig deep burrows.

camouflage: Colors and patterns that help animals blend in with their surroundings. Camouflage helps animals stay safe from enemies.

dormant: Not active. Many trees become dormant so they can survive winter.

hibernate: To spend winter in a deep sleep. Animals hibernate to survive cold weather when there is less food.

icicles: Long, thin pieces of ice. Icicles form when ice melts, drips, and freezes.

dens: Places where bears and other animals live. Bear dens can be in caves, hollow trees, and in piles of leaves.

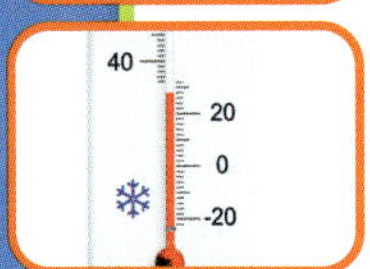

temperature: The measure of how hot or cold something is. A thermometer measures temperature.

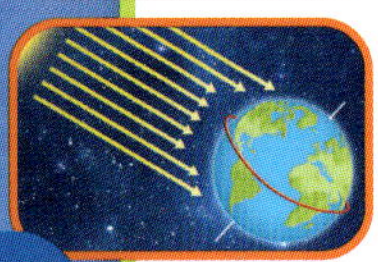

tilts: Leans, tips, or slants to one side. Earth tilts on its axis.

Read More

Earley, Christina. *In the Winter.* New York, NY: Crabtree Publishing, 2023.

Leaf, Christina. *Winter.* Minneapolis, MN: Bellwether Media, 2023.

Murray, Julie. *Winter Adventures.* Minneapolis, MN: Abdo Kids Junior, 2022.

Youssef, Jagger. *Seasons.* New York, NY: PowerKids Press, 2023.

Websites

FACTSURFER

Factsurfer.com gives you a safe, fun way to find more information.

1. Go to www.factsurfer.com.
2. Enter "Winter" into the search box and click 🔍
3. Select your book cover to see a list of related websites.

About the Author

Mari Schuh's love of reading began with cereal boxes at the kitchen table. Today she is the author of hundreds of nonfiction books for beginning readers. Mari lives in the Midwest with her husband and their sassy house rabbit. Learn more about her at marischuh.com.

INDEX

PHOTO CREDITS

The images in this book are reproduced through the courtesy of: Swetlana Wall/Shutterstock Images, cover (top left); Leonid Ikan/Shutterstock Images, cover (top right); Volodymyr TVERDOKHLIB/Shutterstock Images, cover (bottom); Rawpixel.com/Shutterstock Images, title page; Yuriy Boyko_Ukraine/Shutterstock Images, p. 3; Melinda Nagy/Shutterstock Images, p. 4–5; ANURAK PONGPATIMET/Shutterstock Images, p. 4 (circle); sg.photogram/Shutterstock Images, p. 6 (top); Tomas Ragina/Shutterstock Images, p. 6 (bottom); rui vale sousa/Shutterstock Images, p. 7 (top); Standret/Shutterstock Images, p. 7 (bottom); Mihai_Andritoiu/Shutterstock Images, p. 8 (all four seasons); FamVeld/Shutterstock Images, p. 10; Sergey Novikov/Shutterstock Images, p. 10 (bottom); Mirelle/Shutterstock Images, p. 11; Air Images/Shutterstock Images, p. 12; upslim/Shutterstock Images, p. 12 (circle); VINCENT GIORDANO PHOTO/Shutterstock Images, p. 13 (green mittens); Natalia Siverina/Shutterstock Images, p. 13 (skates); Petr Jilek/Shutterstock Images, p. 13 (sled); vvetc1/Shutterstock Images, p. 13 (boots); teh_z1b/Shutterstock Images, p. 13 (shovel); Guas/Shutterstock Images, p. 13 (stocking cap); Karkas/Shutterstock Images, p. 13 (jacket); kedrov/Shutterstock Images, p. 13 (scarf); MyImages - Micha/Shutterstock Images, p. 13 (snowboard); L-N/Shutterstock Images, p. 14; Owsigor/Shutterstock Images, p. 15; Volodymyr Burdiak/Shutterstock Images, p. 16; Tony Campbell/Shutterstock Images, p. 17 (top); vagonik/Shutterstock Images, p. 17 (bottom); Vladimir Salman/Shutterstock Images, p. 18; Beautiful landscape/Shutterstock Images, p. 19; ANURAK PONGPATIMET/Shutterstock Images, p. 20; Tainar/Shutterstock Images, p. 21 (top); WoodysPhotos/Shutterstock Images, p. 21 (bottom); L-N/Shutterstock Images, p. 22 (camouflage); rui vale sousa/Shutterstock Images, p. 22 (icicles); Owsigor/Shutterstock Images, p. 22 (burrows); Skylines/Shutterstock Images, p. 22 (blizzard); Tomas Ragina/Shutterstock Images, p. 22 (temperature); Vladimir Salman/Shutterstock Images, p. 22 (dormant); MM.Wildlifephotos/Shutterstock Images, p. 22 (hibernate); Lars Ove Jonsson/Shutterstock Images, p. 22 (dens); Jeanette Fellows/Shutterstock Images, p. 23.